# DIEFENBAKER

**THE CANADIAN POLITICAL CARTOON SERIES**
Edited by Thad McIlroy

**A ROSE IS A ROSE**
**A Tribute to Pierre Elliott Trudeau**

**DIEFENBAKER**
**Remembering the Chief**

# DIEFENBAKER
## REMEMBERING THE CHIEF

**Introduction by
JACK MACLEOD**

**Edited by
THAD McILROY**

AN ARCADIA HOUSE BOOK

DOUBLEDAY CANADA LIMITED, TORONTO, CANADA
DOUBLEDAY and COMPANY, INC., GARDEN CITY, NEW YORK
1984

**AN ARCADIA HOUSE BOOK**
Jack Jensen
Thad McIlroy
Garfield Reeves-Stevens

**Diefenbaker**
**Remembering the Chief**
**A Nostalgic Tribute in**
**Cartoons and Quotes**
Copyright © 1984 by Arcadia House Inc.
All rights reserved.

**CANADIAN CATALOGUING IN PUBLICATION DATA**

Main entry under title:

Diefenbaker: remembering the chief

Text consists of quotes by Diefenbaker.
ISBN 0-385-19789-6 (bound). — 0-385-19790-X (pbk.)

1. Diefenbaker, John G., 1895-1979 — Cartoons, satire, etc. 2. Canada — Politics and government — 1957-1963 — Caricatures and cartoons. 3. Canadian wit and humor, Pictorial. I. Diefenbaker, John G., 1895-1979. II. McIlroy, Thad, 1956-

FC616.D5305 1984     971.064'2'0924     C84-098867-2
F1034.3.D5D53 1974

Library of Congress Catalog Card Number: 84-10263

Typeset by
JAY TEE GRAPHICS LIMITED
Printed and bound in Canada by
IMPRIMERIE GAGNE LTEE

# CONTENTS

*FRANKLIN*
*THE GLOBE & MAIL, TORONTO*

# FOREWORD

This museum appreciates the cartoons of John G. Diefenbaker for their wit and insight, much as did the editorial pages that originally showcased them.

With a few deft strokes and even fewer words, they capture not just a man, but Canadian political and social conflicts over more than thirty years. Of course his features and gestures delighted the cartoonists of his era. They lost themselves to the exaggeration that is at the heart of caricature. But his deeply held beliefs and political convictions in a time of rapid social change gave them the issues on which to focus.

We tend to think of political cartoons as ephemeral; of interest only as long as the issue portrayed is topical. Yet these cartoons, taken as a whole, provide a remarkable portrait of the life and times of Canada's 13th prime minister.

I'm always intrigued that young school children, unfamiliar with the people or events portrayed, can tell what "the Chief" was like. In particular, they sense the passion and zeal with which he pursued his goals (though not always expressed in those words). They also note with childish glee, not unlike his own, that he made life difficult for those who opposed him.

Children are quick to recognize cruelty — sometimes the savage attack of the artist's pen is truly felt! They go beyond making a point about a "tough" issue. Despite this, the cartoonists saw fit to present them to Diefenbaker, or in many cases he requested them. Clearly they were enjoyed by the subject.

They do continue to instruct and delight. How amused people are now, in the days of a 76¢ Canadian dollar, to see the Diefenbuck worth a mere 92 1/2¢ American, or those cartoons on the subject of patronage or factions within the Cabinet!

My own favorite is still the Ed Franklin cartoon of Dief as the rising sun over Prince Albert. The symbolism reveals a truth that is poetic in its brevity.

— *Sharon Mitchell*
Director
The Right Honourable
John G. Diefenbaker Centre
August, 1984

# PREFACE

A reader generally reads the preface before the body of the book, but the writer prepares the preface as the last item of business.

I am writing this after spending considerable time completely immersed in the remarkable life and times of a unique Canadian, John George Diefenbaker.

Though I can say that I've lived through much of his times, I would have a hard time convincing you that I appreciated them: I was nine months old when John Diefenbaker became Prime Minister in June, 1957. I came of age during the Pierre Trudeau reign, and naturally enough made Trudeau the subject of the first volume in this series, called *A Rose is a Rose*. Preparing *Diefenbaker: Remembering the Chief* has been an education. Trudeau spoke gently of Diefenbaker, and seemed genuinely to mourn his passing. The only times Diefenbaker spoke gently of Trudeau were after his wedding, and once on his birthday. Generally he referred to him as the new Machiavelli. They were very different men.

In these days of plastic politics, where the image is the message, what are we to make of a man who campaigned with the slogan, "We have an appointment with destiny," who spoke for the "little people," the "ordinary Canadians?"

"I don't campaign," Diefenbaker said in 1965, "I just visit with the people." I find it impossible to imagine these words coming from the mouth of Pierre Trudeau. Though perhaps we are witnessing a change in the nature of Canadian politics. As I write this, it is the new Conservative leader, Brian Mulroney who, the newspapers say, is running a "Diefenbaker-style campaign."

The time to shun and forget John Diefenbaker has passed. The time to remember him and to celebrate his achievements has arrived (with apologies to the many people in Western Canada who have kept his memory very much alive).

And so I invite you to visit the Diefenbaker years — be it to reacquaint yourself or to see them for the first time. If a picture is worth a thousand words, then I'd rate a political cartoon at about five thousand. You'll find more than ninety of them here to amuse and inform you. Many have been reproduced from originals held at the Diefenbaker Archives in Saskatoon; Diefenbaker was one of the cartoonists' biggest fans.

And please pause along the way to read the quotations. What politician do you know of today who could get away with saying, "Nothing I ever do is political" (JGD, 1978)?

— *Thad McIlroy*
*Toronto*
*August, 1984*

# ACKNOWLEDGMENTS

Special thanks are due to the staff of The Right Honourable John G. Diefenbaker Centre, who provided invaluable assistance with the research for this book: the director, Sharon Mitchell; education officer, Diane Bryden; secretary, Helen Aikenhead; and the student assistants, who never flinched in the face of "just one more thing:" Nancy Noble, Sarah Spafford, Cheryl Holmlund, Ian Sutherland and Sandra Walter.

This book is for Michael Lomer and Heather Robertson, for their exceptional kindness and support.

# INTRODUCTION

All the world loves a rogue. In the tradition of Sir John A., John George Diefenbaker was that: unique, flamboyant, erratic, unrepentant, a renegade, a maverick. Just as Canada's first prime minister said of himself, "The voters prefer John A. drunk to George Brown sober," it could be said that the voters preferred John G. fulminating to Lester Pearson dithering.

With all the odds stacked against him, Mr. Diefenbaker rose to the office of prime minister and won, in 1958, the biggest parliamentary majority of any Canadian leader. More importantly, he cloaked himself in legend. Some said he was our closest approximation to a twentieth century Abe Lincoln.

Controversy always surrounded him like hounds around a bear. To some he was a hero, a saviour; to others he was a droll con man and anathema. He had enemies in his own party, even in his own cabinets. The "establishment" shunned him: President John F. Kennedy was hostile to him; the media began to scorn him during his second administration; and after 1964 there was open rebellion in the Conservative ranks. "Everyone is against me," he used to say, "except the people."

He was not wrong. Seldom did a politician achieve such an electric rapport with his followers and become so much cherished by the ordinary "little people" who were quick to wink at his faults and loyal in their affection for one who spoke for them.

Diefenbaker was, above all, a populist. None of the other orthodox labels seemed adequate to fit him. Tory? Red Tory? Prairie radical? Enemy of the privileged? Self-serving manipulator of the neglected masses? Egomaniac? Strident champion of the underdog? All of the above? Whatever. If a populist is one who strikes deep and responsive chords in the hearts of ordinary folks, articulates their resentments and grievances, and attempts to protect their interests, John G. Diefenbaker was the Canadian populist *par excellence* of recent decades. Surely our somewhat narrow and elitist political culture has reason to prize a genuine tribune of the little guy.

He reached the pinnacle, but none of it came easily. His modest pioneering family provided no silver spoon for young John's mouth. Still, his gift for rotund rhetoric and his nimble legal mind won him many notable court cases, often on behalf of ordinary and impecunious clients. His victories in court, however, were offset by a dismaying series of early political losses. Later, some said he was paranoid, but we must recall that the future prime minister was a Tory in Saskatchewan when the prairie Conservatives were at best an endangered species. In his early years, Dief lost enough elections at almost every level to have crushed a lesser man. In 1925 and in 1926 he ran federally in Prince Albert against a chap named Mackenzie King; guess who won? Dief was defeated in a provincial riding in 1929, defeated in a mayoralty race in Prince Albert in 1933, defeated again in a provincial seat in 1938. Political doors seemed to be slammed against him everywhere.

But the word "quit" was not in his vocabulary. When in 1940 he finally won in the federal constituency of Lake Centre, he came up against the tough Liberal machine of Jimmy Gardiner and found that his seat was "Jimmymandered" into jeopardy in a raw way, but endured until a further "adjustment" of boundaries totally abolished his riding. Undaunted, he ran in Prince Albert in the federal election of 1953 on the immodest but successful slogan of:

"Not a partisan cry but a national need." No one ever accused him of being shy about self-promotion.

The Gardiner machine, trying to torment him further, bought the house next to the Diefenbakers' and turned it into a home for unwed mothers. Saskatchewan politics were seldom delicate. If he could be vengeful and often vilify opponents, it was not that he was any stranger to adversity himself.

Diefenbaker's surprising survival was grudgingly admired but not much rewarded within the eastern wing of his own party. Some, frankly, regarded him as an ambitious rustic from the wrong side of the political tracks. He contested the Conservative federal leadership in 1942 and ran third; in 1948 a party convention again froze him out and gave the national leadership to the dapper but dreary George Drew. When Drew proved to have little appeal among voters beyond Ontario, the party finally, if reluctantly, accepted John G. as their leader in 1956. Canadian politics would never be the same.

It was not so much the Conservative party as the Diefenbaker party that astoundingly upset the Liberals in the

election of 1957. The dominant Grits had been the sun party to the pale Conservative moon in Ottawa for most of the twentieth century. From 1896 to 1957, the Liberals serenely held office for 46 of those 61 years, and for an unbroken period of 22 years prior to 1957. Liberal government apparently was "normal" government, and the Grits were known as "The Government Party." There were many reasons for this, not the least of which included R.B. Bennett's misfortune of being in office during the worst of the depression of the '30s, plus the Conservative's advocacy of conscription in both World Wars, a policy which was repugnant to most Quebeçois.

But there was another major factor. Consider: how many leaders did the Liberal party of Canada have between 1887 and 1948? Two: Laurier and King, one French and one English — Canadian in artful alternation. Meanwhile, back at the Conservative ranch, the Tories were churning through eleven different leaders . . . not one of whom was a francophone. Small wonder that the exalted Grits sailed into most federal elections with the happy certainty of some 70 of the 75 Quebec seats in their pocket before the writs were issued. Small wonder that the Liberals were the entrenched "natural majority" party, usually implacable, arrogant, and casually in control.

John G. Diefenbaker changed all that, and changed it abruptly. In June of 1957, Dief the Chief accomplished the seemingly impossible and ousted the Grits, some said (with pardonable exaggeration), single-handedly. Quebec gave him only 9 seats in that election, but he toppled St. Laurent, became prime minister of a fresh minority government, and in 1958 swept 50 of the 75 Quebec seats to win by a stunning landslide of 208 seats to the Liberal's 48 (others, 9). It was the most overwhelming victory in national political history, and Diefenbaker's supreme moment.

However, he could not hold that moment for long. His government was reduced to a minority in 1962, then defeated by Lester B. Pearson's Liberals in '63. Why? Why did Diefenbaker fail to consolidate his power and establish the Conservatives as the "dominant" party?

It was not because he failed to implement a considerable quantity of innovative legislation. His "Vision of the North" initially captured the popular imagination much as had Sir John A.'s National Policy in the previous century. Diefenbaker's 1957-1958 minority government in particular passed an impressive spate of positive bills, and after 1958 he had many real accomplishments to his credit. Alvin Hamilton, the best brain in his cabinet, and Merril Menzies, his principal economic advisor, helped him to compile a solid policy record: the "Roads to Resources" program; cost-sharing for a national hospital insurance scheme, significant increases in welfare programs such as pensions and assistance to farmers; huge wheat sales to China; the South Saskatchewan River Dam project; and the Act probably closest to his heart, the 1960 Bill of Rights.

But "One Canada" became his major theme, and part of his downfall. "Un-hyphenated" Canadianism did not sit well with certain proponents of multi-culturalism, and certainly not with most French-Canadians, who instinctively felt slighted. Inability or unwillingness to find francophones to fill senior cabinet portfolios, plus his reluctance to acknowledge the duality of Canada or the special sensitivities of Quebec, led that province to abandon him abruptly in the elections of 1962 and 1963 and to move back into the Liberal fold.

Moreover, economics was not the Chief's long suit. Recession, unemployment, and the slide of the Canadian dollar led to rude jokes about "Diefenbucks." Defence policy also proved troublesome. He accepted Bomarc missiles for Canada but declined to equip them with nuclear warheads. This was like buying a car without an engine and led to serious schisms within the cabinet, culminating in the resignation of Douglas Harkness, the Minister of Defence. After the 1962 election, mutterings of discontent and open revolt became increasingly obvious, both within the cabinet and the party.

Administration, in short, was not Diefenbaker's forte. He was superb in the House of Commons, a devoted and skilful parliamentarian, but even there he often seemed more eager to tear strips off Pearson and the hated Liberals than to placate his own caucus or focus his own policy thrusts. Some said that as Prime Minister he sounded more like a slashing leader of the opposition. Indignation and frequent bursts of outrage characterized his verbal abuse of his critics. A conciliator, he was not. He saw only two ways: his way, and error—and woe betide those who were in error, for they would suffer the lash of his tongue and his scornful wit.

It was on the hustings that Dief the Chief was at his best. Here he was a cartoonist's delight (and no one enjoyed the cartoons more than he did—all praise be to a man who can laugh at himself). A detractor once said of John G. as campaigner that "the voice is the voice of God, but the face is the face of Bugs Bunny." Yet somehow on the platform it all came together, it all worked, at least for the faithful. He was part adversarial lawyer, part thespian, part evangelical denunciator of Grit evil, and all politician. With stabbing gestures, quivering jowls, blistering righteousness and blazing eyes, he resembled a galleon in full sail running before a strong wind of his own making. Dief, in full oratorical flight, was an unforgettable spectacle of remarkable if unpredictable power, playing his audience like Glenn Gould playing the piano, wringing the maximum out of every theme and variation.

If this tended toward the politics of bluster and showbiz, the other side of his style was displayed through the common touch of "mainstreeting," an art which he perfected and made part of our vocabulary. In his home constituency these events were seldom orchestrated, more often spontaneous, frequently nudged along by his friend and constituency association president, Dick Spencer. I watched him on more than one occasion. The Old Chieftain would simply take a walk, and people would come to him. Some would hang back at first, timid about approaching, but their wide glowing eyes gave eloquent signals that they would soon edge forward to ask for an autograph, or merely shake hands and say hello, so that they could tell their grandchildren that they had once spoken to a living legend. The Chief's response was always quick and warm. "Makarchuk? I knew your father. How's your aunt Ada?" In mainstreeting with Dief you got the feeling that beyond the TV studios of Ottawa or Toronto there was something plain and dependable and, well, fundamentally decent about the people who live in this country. It was curiously reassuring about the sometimes demented

nature of our now mainly electronic political process. On his casual walkabouts, Diefenbaker was not so much "pressing the flesh" as he was touching the nerves.

And that, in a sense, is what John G. Diefenbaker did to millions of Canadians; with his exuberant qualities and abundant shortcomings, he touched us. His funeral cortège by train from Ottawa to Saskatoon in August of 1979 was a prolonged and self-consciously planned cross-country extravaganza, larger than life.

But then, so was he.

*— Jack MacLeod*
(Jack MacLeod is a professor of politics at the University of Toronto, and author of two novels, *Zinger and Me,* and *Going Grand.*)

# THE MAN FROM PRINCE ALBERT

*"And now — something for me."*

GRASSICK
TORONTO TELEGRAM, DECEMBER 11, 1956

"**I first ventured** into politics in 1920 by contesting the office of councillor in the village of Wakaw (Saskatchewan). I do not exactly remember why I decided to run."

*— John Diefenbaker*
*from Carolyn Weir*
Diefenbaker: A Pictorial Tribute

"**I have but** one love, Canada. One purpose, it's greatness. One aim, unity from the Atlantic to the Pacific."

*— John Diefenbaker*
*Ottawa, Ontario, December 13, 1956*
*(in his election speech at the Conservative leadership convention)*

"**On January 14,** 1957, he won (the leadership of the Conservative Party) on the first ballot, with 774 votes, to Donald Fleming's 393, and Davie Fulton's 119."

*— Donald Creighton*
The Forked Road

"**The full meaning** of the words 'Diefenbaker Revolution' emerges when it is realized that some of the doubts about Mr. Diefenbaker's qualities of leadership were entertained, singly and in combination, by virtually every one of the then leading members of the party. With two or three exceptions, every member of the Conservative front bench in the House of Commons was opposed to Mr. Diefenbaker. Mr. Drew was known not to favour him as a successor. Before balloting began, the president of the Progressive Conservative Association of Canada openly attacked him. It was announced that the acting leader of the party supported Mr. Fleming. A 'Stop Diefenbaker' movement developed and was associated with an attempt to draft the president of the University of Toronto, Sidney Smith, as leader."

*— John Meisel*
The Canadian General Election of 1957

"**. . . the leadership was** coming to John (in 1957) if persistence, hard work and speaking ability deserve a reward — but his organization would have given him the edge in any event."

*— John Bracken*
*Former Conservative Party leader*
*from John Kendle*
John Bracken: A Political Biography

"**I would have** retired from politics in 1952 if my constituency had not for the third time running been gerrymandered in the redistribution."

*— John Diefenbaker*
*Diefenbaker had been a member of Parliament for 12 years by 1952. That year's redistribution simply removed the riding of Lake Centre. Instead of retiring, an outraged Diefenbaker ran successfully in Prince Albert, which he continued to represent until his death.*
One Canada: Volume 1

"**Jimmymander**"

*— John Diefenbaker*
*A play on 'gerrymander', as Jimmy Gardiner kept readjusting the boundaries of Diefenbaker's Lake Centre riding, in an effort to defeat him.*

*KAMIENSKI*
*WINNIPEG TRIBUNE*

*This cartoon is from the Diefenbaker Archives. It is undated. Though it probably appeared in 1957 or 1958, I felt it aptly illustrated the situation described above.*

**"What's a million?"**
— *John Diefenbaker accused C.D. Howe of using this line during the 1945 debates on war estimates. Howe had in fact said, "A million dollars from the War Appropriations Bill would not be a very important matter," which was true, as the budget was $1.4 billion. Diefenbaker continued to use the line as an example of Liberal arrogance.*
*from Robert Bothwell and William Kilbourn*
C.D. Howe: A Biography

**"The honourable member** has spoken from the sewer of his own mind."
— *C.D. Howe to Diefenbaker, when charged that he would use favouritism in granting export permits*
*February, 1948.*
*from Leslie Roberts* C.D.: The Life & Times of Clarence Decatur Howe

**"C.D. Howe had** no more use for Parliament than Satan has for Heaven."
— *John Diefenbaker*
One Canada: Volume 2

**"His law practice** was successful from the start. . . His first murder case, tried at Humboldt on his twenty-fourth birthday, involved the defence of a farmer accused of attempting to kill a neighbour with a shotgun. The farmer's only excuse was that he thought the victim was a wolf, and the judge issued a strong charge, all but directing the jury to convict. Instead, the verdict was not guilty.

"The astonished young lawyer met the jury foreman a few days later and asked him how the decision was reached. 'Well,' was the reply, 'we talked it over, and somebody said: "After all, it's the kid's first case." Then somebody else said: "And it's his birthday too!" That settled it. We all voted for acquittal.' "
— *Peter C. Newman*
Renegade in Power

**"Pearson:** 205
**Elephants:** 500
**Diefenbaker:** 1,200"
— *In the 1953 election campaign, on a visit to Moncton, Diefenbaker was said to have outdrawn both Pearson and the visiting King Brothers and Christiana Circus.*
*from Patrick Nicholson*
Vision and Indecision

**"In 1956, John** Diefenbaker looked much younger than his then sixty-two years. There was no grey in his hair, and he had a gauche, almost timid way about him in his first contacts with people. But he laughed easily and made friends wherever he went. He had a sense of humor and a natural wit, and these pleasantly contrasted with the pomposity and coldness of some of his fellow Tories in Parliament."
— *Pierre Sevigny*
This Game of Politics

**"It'll be a** dam sight sooner if John is elected."
— *slogan for the 1945 election campaign (referring to the South Saskatchewan dam, coined by Elmer Diefenbaker, his brother)*

**"Diefenbaker might well** be the choice. He is a second Arthur Meighen in style, satire, etc. Also very hard working and informed. His name will be against him. . ."
— *Mackenzie King reflecting on possible choices for new Conservative Party leader*
*July 19, 1948*
*from* The Mackenzie King Record: Vol. IV
*(George Drew won on October 3, 1948)*

*KUCH*
*WINNIPEG FREE PRESS, AUGUST 27, 1954*

*This is the earliest Diefenbaker cartoon obtainable from the Diefenbaker Archives.*

*"Election stakes: backing the same loser."*

# "WE HAVE AN APPOINTMENT WITH DESTINY"

## Election — 1957

*BEATON*
*VANCOUVER PROVINCE, FEBRUARY 25, 1958*

"**If you work** hard enough, there's no reason why you shouldn't."
— *Diefenbaker's mother, Mary, when at the age of six he told her he one day intended to be prime minister*
*from Patrick Nicholson*
Vision and Indecision

"**Yes, ladies and** gentlemen, I give you Mr. Studebaker."
— *an anecdote of Diefenbaker's early years illustrating the problem he often had with his name*
*from Patrick Nicholson*
Vision and Indecision

"**Give us your** confidence and I promise we will give you satisfaction."
— *John Diefenbaker*
*Ste. Germaine, Quebec, May 30, 1957*
*from* Quotations from Chairman Diefenbaker

"**We have an** appointment with destiny."
— *John Diefenbaker*
*(slogan used in the 1957 campaign)*

"**It's time for** a Diefenbaker government."
— *1957 campaign slogan written by Dalton Camp*
*from John Robert Columbo*
Colombo's Canadian Quotations
*(The Conservatives had been out of power for so long that a decision was made to emphasize the candidate and not the party in this election. Only in small type on the bottom of Diefenbaker campaign material did the words appear:*
*"Published by the Progressive Conservative Party of Canada.")*

"**C.D. Howe and** some others . . . treated the feverish activities and old-time political orations of that Prairie Savonarola, John Diefenbaker, who was conducting an almost one-man campaign, with something approaching amused contempt."
— *Lester B. Pearson*
Mike: Volume 3

"**Not since the** days of John A. Macdonald had the Conservative Party produced a leader with the magnetic personality of John Diefenbaker."
— *Heath Macquarrie*
The Conservative Party

"**Someone has given** me a copy of the Prime Minister's speech. I don't know why they bothered. There's nothing in it."
— *John Diefenbaker campaigning in Stratford, Ontario in 1957*

*GRASSICK*
*TORONTO TELEGRAM, MAY 24, 1957*

"**Mr. Howe determines** what is to be done. Mr. St. Laurent agrees. The rest of the cabinet says 'me too' and the 187 other Liberals add 'amen.' "

— *John Diefenbaker*
*New Glasgow, N.B., April 30, 1957*

"**Newspapers covering John** Diefenbaker's election tour are going to have to lay on their reporters in relays, like the pony express. As each man is relieved, burned out, he will need to be sent before a medical board which will determine the extent of the damage to his system and say if it is repairable. It is hoped that not too many will have to be destroyed."

— *George Bain*
The Globe & Mail,
*April 25, 1957*
*from the Diefenbaker scrapbook, April, 1957*
*Diefenbaker was famous for the number of stops he could fit into a campaign.*

" '**In his own** way Diefenbaker is a pretty boy, he looks good — nice hair, nice eyes — he speaks well, he is a good orator, presents himself well. He almost looks like a man, which is saying something for a Conservative. I like him. He's got something. What you should do is sell him as a man. Forget about the Conservatives, forget about the party, but build that man up. Now, what he said about Confederation is what needs to be said. Build him up!' I remember his words. 'You have got to make him a combination of Churchill, de Gaulle, Moses, God, and maybe the Devil, because he has got a bit of that in him. This combination usually wins votes. Do that.' "

— *Pierre Sevigny recalling Maurice Duplessis' decision to support Diefenbaker in the 1957 election*
*quoted in* Diefenbaker: Leadership Gained

"**It is a** deep inspiration for me to see this vast audience. This is the kind of thing that gives me the strength to continue to work on behalf of the average men and women of this country. From the bottom of my heart I thank you. I won't let you down."

— *John Diefenbaker*
*Vancouver, B.C., May 24, 1957*

"**All Canadians will** wish the Prime Minister a pleasant and restful holiday in the Bahamas. Whatever anyone may think of the policies of his government, no one will deny that he has worked strenuously in the few months he has been in office."

— *from the* Charlottetown Guardian
*December 30, 1957*

*CHAMBERS*
*HALIFAX CHRONICLE HERALD, OCTOBER 11, 1957*

*"Shades of the First Elizabeth"*

*"All in favor?"*

*GRASSICK*
*TORONTO TELEGRAM, NOVEMBER 1, 1957*

"After you."

**"His language was** a splendid artifice. His every parliamentary appearance let loose a hundred verbal balloons, tangled together in wild confusion . . . it was the best show in town."

— *Peter C. Newman*
Distemper of our Times

**"There are more** votes on Main Street than Bay Street."

— *John Diefenbaker*
*(during the 1958 election campaign)*

*ANONYMOUS*
*REGINA LEADER POST, JANUARY 23, 1958*

CALLAN
THE TORONTO STAR, JANUARY 31, 1958

TING
LONDON FREE PRESS, FEBRUARY 2, 1958

"Captain Diefenbaker: I found the position intolerable."

KUCH
WINNIPEG FREE PRESS, FEBRUARY 4, 1958

This was one of Diefenbaker's favorite early cartoons. Critics felt that the Diefenbaker minority government
had functioned well, and that an election was unnecessary.

". . . it was Diefenbaker's northern vision that captured the national imagination."
> — *Robert Bothwell, Ian Drummond and*
> *John English*
> Canada Since 1945

"One Canada, one Canada, where Canadians will have preserved to them the control of their own economic and political destiny. Sir John A. Macdonald gave his life to this party. He opened the west. He saw Canada from east to west. I see a new Canada — a Canada of the North!"
> — *John Diefenbaker*
> *Winnipeg, Manitoba, February 12, 1958*
> *from* Quotations from Chairman Diefenbaker

"In emphasizing the question of northern development and northern vision, I advocated a twentieth-century equivalent of Sir John A. Macdonald's national policy, a uniquely Canadian economic dream."
> — *John Diefenbaker*
> One Canada: Volume 2

"I haven't yet learned the art of having someone else write my speeches."
> — *John Diefenbaker*
> *Canadian Press interview, June 21, 1958*

*KUCH*
*WINNIPEG FREE PRESS, APRIL 2, 1958*

*"Surrealism in Politics: 'That way is a vision. The vision is a plan and a program.'*
*(The Prime Minister)"*

**"Apparently I just** can't pronounce French well while talking. An English-speaking friend joked to me, 'I love to hear you talk French on television. When you do, every English-speaking person in the audience, who doesn't know a word of French, can understand every word you say.' "

*— John Diefenbaker*
*from* Quotations from Chairman Diefenbaker

**"I haven't practiced** my French. It's just that you are starting to understand it better."

*— John Diefenbaker*
*St. Hyacinthe, Quebec, August 23, 1965*
*from* Quotations from Chairman Diefenbaker

**"His knowledge of** French was very good."

*— Jean Drapeau*
*from Brian McKenna and Susan Purcell*
Drapeau

**"Prime Minister Diefenbaker,** one of Canada's best-known students of the French language, tacitly admitted Friday he has problems with off-the-cuff talks in French.

"He declined to speak in French while attending the opening of the fall assizes at the Quebec court house, recalling an embarrassing moment during an impromptu French talk in the Gaspé Peninsula.

" 'At the beginning of a little speech while I was trying to improvise in French, all seemed to be going well, when suddenly I got stuck with an English word of which I did not know the French equivalent.

" 'I turned to a friend and not realizing that I was in front of microphones, I asked him in English: "How in the h... do you translate 'panorama' in French?' "

"Mr. Diefenbaker did not say whether he has since learned that the word 'panorama' is the same in French and English."

*— from a Canadian Press story "P.M.*
*admits his French needs help"*
*September 10, 1960, from the Diefenbaker*
*Scrapbook, September, 1960*

**"Canada was conceived** by men of two different but equally rich cultures, of two distinctive communities. Bilingualism and biculturalism are facts of Canadian life that cannot — and should not — be hidden or avoided. They are important, even vital, to Canada as a nation. But they are assets, not liabilities; positive factors, not negative ones."

*— John Diefenbaker in a letter, 1964*
One Canada, Volume 3

*HUNTER*
*LE SOLEIL (QUEBEC), MARCH 1, 1958*

*"Il en faudra un pour céder . . .!" / "One of them must yield . . .!"*

# ONE CANADA

## Landslide — 1958

*"The Law moves West — 1958"*

*SEBESTYEN*
*SASKATOON STAR-PHOENIX, 1958*

**"I told him:** 'Well, let's leave it as this. One Canada where everybody will live together in harmony.' . . . My God, it was as if I had put a bomb under his seat. He got up and said, 'That's it! Yes. One Canada.' Then, he started right there in front of us all and he said, 'One Canada! What we can build around that slogan!' "
— *Pierre Sevigny on the 1958 election quoted in* Diefenbaker: Leadership Gained

**"Diefenbaker has been** a friend of mine since he entered the House of Commons and, although I still like him personally, I am wondering what kind of government his will prove to be."
— *C.D. Howe in a letter to R.E. Powell September, 1957 from Robert Bothwell and William Kilbourn* C.D. Howe: A Biography

**"Russian newspapers have** hailed the election of John Diefenbaker. Presumably they are encouraged to find another country in which everybody votes for one party.

"Washington foreign experts, on the other hand, are puzzled by the emergence of a man who dares to challenge the United States of America yet still believes in God."

— *Eric Nicol* The *Vancouver Province April 15, 1958 from the Diefenbaker Scrapbook, April, 1958*

" **'Of course I** voted for Mr. Diefenbaker! I thought he was a voice crying in the wilderness against the corruption and arrogance that comes from long holding of power in office, and I thought I would just vote Conservative this one time.

" 'Of course I had no idea they would ever win any seats.' "

— *the wife of a prominent Liberal quoted in* Mike: Volume 3

" 'Conservative is a misnomer when applied to Diefenbaker,' an old guard editorial charged.

"Diefenbaker replied by quoting Tennyson:

" 'He is the true conservative who lops the mouldered branch away.' "

> — The Milwaukee Journal
> *February 2, 1960*
> *from the Diefenbaker scrapbook,*
> *January/February, 1960*

"He's the practical man, the one with crowd appeal."

> — *Yoshito Mizuno, a Japanese*
> *"face-reader" predicting that Diefenbaker*
> *would win the 1958 election*
> *reported by Robert McKeown in*
> Weekend Magazine, *May 17, 1958*

*This little drawing appears in Diefenbaker's scrapbook for May, 1958, stamped "Office of the Secretary of State." Its source is not attributed.*

**"I was aboard** my brother's train for the western parts of both the 1957 and 1958 elections. I saw him do on a national scale what he'd done in Lake Centre nearly 20 years earlier: travel the length and breadth of his trans-continental 'riding' and get to know the people. His phenomenal memory was a help here as it was in the courtroom. I saw it demonstrated at Ituna, Saskatchewan. A World War I veteran whom he hadn't seen for 20 years was at the station where he was speaking during a brief stop. John went over to him immediately, shook his hand and said, 'How are you, Alf?' Everyone was amazed.''
— *Elmer Diefenbaker in ''My Brother John'' which appeared in the* Star Weekly *September 26, 1959 from the Diefenbaker scrapbook, September, 1959*

**"In the western** provinces there was a particularly interesting phenomenon (in the 1958 election). An examination of the return shows that the Liberals and the C.C.F. in their best strongholds mustered as many votes as they had previously. Sometimes more. Yet they went down to defeat. Obviously thousands of young, new votes, and older people who had never bothered to vote before, turned up at the polling places to go on the record for Diefenbaker.''
— *Milton Mackaye* The Saturday Evening Post *August 30, 1958 from the Diefenbaker scrapbook, August, 1958*

**"Having a prime** minister in the riding is a bit like having an industry. It gives you an advantage over other ridings. Look what Diefenbaker did for Prince Albert. Who had heard of Prince Albert?''
— *Jean Croteau, of Sept-Iles, Quebec, discussing whether to vote for Brian Mulroney in 1984 election quoted by Graham Fraser in the* Globe & Mail, *July 24, 1984*

**"I was extraordinarily** fond of fishing as a boy; I still am, as was my father before me. There is a pleasure and, above all, a peace to be enjoyed in fishing beyond anything else I know; it is as if the outside world were forbidden to intrude upon a fisherman's thoughts.''
— *John Diefenbaker* One Canada: Volume 1

**"You've been given** the opportunity to do something for your country. Do not forget the poor and afflicted. Do the best you can as long as you can.''
— *John Diefenbaker recalling his mother Mary's words on election night June 10, 1957* One Canada: Volume 2

*SEBESTYEN SASKATOON STAR-PHOENIX, APRIL 3, 1958*

"I'll bet _we_ put up a better fight against Mr. John and Fred Hadley."

**"Care to test** your sense of humour?

"Just take a look at the cartoon published below. Isn't it witty, penetrating, subtle? Isn't the drawing superb and the draftmanship admirable? No?

"That just shows how wrong you can be.

"It was the best cartoon published in Canada in 1958. For that you have the word of the National Newspaper Award judges. This is an annual competition, covering the various branches of daily journalism, sponsored by the Toronto Men's Press Club.

"At moments like these a Westerner may be excused if he despairs of ever understanding the mysterious East. Or even for wondering if Canada will ever become a nation."

— The Vancouver Sun
*May 27, 1959*

*HUNTER*
*LE SOLEIL (QUEBEC) APRIL 3, 1958*

*"Quebec's traditional fecundity."*

"**The Commonwealth and** all it stands
for, both practically and traditionally, is one
of the glories of our Canadian heritage. It is
the outstanding example in all world history
of amity among free and independent
peoples."

*— John Diefenbaker*
*House of Commons, June 23, 1957*
*from John Munro*
The Wit and Wisdom of John Diefenbaker

*COLLINS*
*MONTREAL GAZETTE, NOVEMBER 4, 1958*

"Mr. Macmillan Meet Mr. Diefenbaker."

"Mr. Diefenbaker I presume?"

In November 1958, Diefenbaker set out on a tour of the Commonwealth that included fourteen countries in six weeks.

CHAMBERS
HALIFAX CHRONICLE HERALD, DECEMBER 3, 1958

"*Let Mr. Diefenbaker take care of his problems and you take care of yours.*"

CLARK
*SYNDICATED, NOVEMBER 24, 1958*

**"Within a few** months of joining the *Star*, (Macpherson) produced a caricature of Prime Minister John Diefenbaker as Marie Antoinette that was regarded instantly as a classic. Macpherson once said that, in fact, he had agreed with the political decision to scrap Canada's Arrow military jet and 1,500 jobs in favour of buying US aircraft.

" 'Even though he was correct, his attitude was wrong' Macpherson explained. 'If a man is correct but his attitude is wrong, pick on his attitude.' "

— *Peter Desbarats and Terry Mosher*
The Hecklers

*MACPHERSON*
*THE TORONTO STAR, MARCH 28, 1959*

"*Let them eat cake.*"

**"The 1958 landslide** was more a referendum than an election, with Diefenbaker the triumphant issue and almost no national divisions. Only Newfoundland stayed Liberal."

— *Desmond Morton*
A Short History of Canada

**"I have never** been able to understand why Mr. Diefenbaker was so cranky and ungenerous to Newfoundland, unless it was the fact that when he swept Canada, almost from stem to stern, Newfoundland stood out and gave him only two of its seven seats. Perhaps he never forgave us for that."

— *Joey Smallwood*
I Chose Canada

*TING*
*LONDON FREE PRESS, 1959*

*"Alvin, you're goofin' it all up!"*

MACPHERSON
THE TORONTO STAR, MARCH, 1959

"**He did speak** strongly and persuasively for the western farmer and for the 'little man' everywhere. He was such an actor and he so often bent facts to suit his role that he put me off, but I believe he was sincere in his attacks on Bay Street and in his defence of the weak in society. Furthermore, he was a terrific campaigner. I don't think he ever recognized the line between campaigning for votes and running the country, but he was a spellbinder on the platform, mixing indignation, vision, and wit into a powerful brew."

*— David Lewis*
The Good Fight

"**I have never** been able to understand or appreciate the appeal that Mr. Diefenbaker has on television. I am forced to believe that he has an appeal. He has none for me. . . I like people to be consecutive and orderly and finish their sentences and know what they are talking about. I could never understand why he gets all the publicity he does, because he never says anything. People say he is a great performer, but you know, I have always preferred opera to rock!"

*— J.W. Pickersgill*
*quoted in* Diefenbaker: Leadership Gained

*BARRON*
*VICTORIA TIMES, JANUARY 5, 1960*

*"Just remember, it's you that's saying everything is Jim Dandy . . . not me . . ."*

"**Like other Canadian** administrations, the Diefenbaker government loved royal commissions."
— *Robert Bothwell, Ian Drummond and*
*John English*
Canada Since 1945

"**It is easy** to talk of extra spending, but sometimes it is hard to find anything useful to spend it on. And compared to the St. Laurent administration, the Diefenbaker government was certainly an ingenious and imaginative spender!"
— *Robert Bothwell, Ian Drummond and*
*John English*
Canada Since 1945

*MACPHERSON*
*TORONTO STAR, APRIL 19, 1960*

*"Tardy Bunny"*

"**As long as** I am Prime Minister this
government will not rest while one
Canadian remains out of work. No one will
be allowed to suffer."
*— John Diefenbaker*
*Television interview, May 4, 1958*
*from* Quotations from Chairman Diefenbaker

"**Poverty is a** passport to prison."
*— John Diefenbaker*
*from J. Allan Ross*
Grassroots Prime Minister

*KUCH*
*WINNIPEG FREE PRESS, MAY 27, 1960*

"I have a little shadow."

"**I am a** Canadian, a free Canadian, free to speak without fear, free to worship God in my own way, free to stand for what I think right, free to oppose what I believe wrong, free to choose those who shall govern my country. This heritage of freedom I pledge to uphold for myself and mankind."

*— John Diefenbaker*
*House of Commons*
*July 1, 1960*
*(from a speech made in reference*
*to the Bill of Rights)*

" **'The secret of** freedom is a brave heart.' It was true when Pericles uttered those words. It is true today."

*— John Diefenbaker*
*Speech to the Canadian Bar Association*
*Winnipeg, September 1, 1961*

"**My basic social** philosophy is that governments should not forget the average man and woman."

*— John Diefenbaker*
The Nation's Business
*March 14, 1962*

"**But I am** convinced that in the perspective of history, John Diefenbaker will be remembered as a man who sincerely tried to improve the lot of the average Canadian. Hospital insurance, the South Saskatchewan Dam and the Canadian Bill of Rights are landmarks to show he did not try in vain."

*— Tommy Douglas*
The Globe & Mail
*August 17, 1979*

*MACPHERSON*
*THE TORONTO STAR, AUGUST 1960*

*"Oh, wouldn't it be luverly?"*

"**It is hard** to describe Mr. Khrushchev. He alternates between carrots and clubs, between sneers and smiles, to which he has now added shoes. He is most unusual, most unpredictable."

*— John Diefenbaker*
*Ottawa, October 22, 1960*
*from* Quotations from Chairman Diefenbaker

"**They said I** shouldn't annoy Mr. Khrushchev. I don't want to annoy him. All I want him to do is give people the same freedom as others. He made his speech asking Britain and France why they have not ended colonialism. I said to him, 'Physician, heal thyself.' "

*— John Diefenbaker*
*Montreal, Quebec, June 11, 1962*
*from* Quotations from Chairman Diefenbaker

"**We are not** here in this Assembly to win wars of propaganda. We are here to win victories for peace."

*— John Diefenbaker*
*Speech to the United Nations*
*General Assembly*
*September 26, 1960*

"**There will be** no second prizes in the next world war."

*— John Diefenbaker*
*May 23, 1967*
*from John Munro*
The Wit and Wisdom of John Diefenbaker

*McNALLY*
*MONTREAL STAR, SEPTEMBER, 1960*

*"Who's he?"*

"**As Prince Albert** goes, so goes the
nation."

*— John Diefenbaker*
*Prince Albert, Sask., April 7, 1973*
*from* Quotations from Chairman Diefenbaker

*SEBESTYEN*
*SASKATOON STAR-PHOENIX, OCTOBER, 1960*

*"Let's see, Diefenbaker . . . Diefenbaker . . . no, that name is not on the guest list!"*

"**Today's lesson: How** to get elected president of the United States, prime minister of Canada, premier of Quebec or mayor of Montreal . . .

"By present odds, if your name happens to be John or any variation thereof, you're a virtual shoo-in.

"There's John F. Kennedy, John G. Diefenbaker, Jean Lesage and Jean Drapeau as irrefutable evidence of the theory."
*— Bill Bantey*
The Montreal Gazette
*November 14, 1960*
*from the Diefenbaker Scrapbook,*
*November, 1960*

*LaPALME*
*LA PRESSE (MONTREAL), OCTOBER 29, 1960*

*Translated literally, the caption reads "The people are right." The French caption is a pun, as "the people" is "les gens."*

*"Les gens ont raison."* / *"The people are right."*

**"I'm not anti-American.** The very
thought is repugnant to me."
— *John Diefenbaker*
*August 5, 1957*
*from Margaret Wente*
I Never Say Anything Provocative

**"A Diefenbaker-Kennedy** meeting in
May of 1961 had proceeded harmoniously;
but Kennedy had inadvertently left behind
one of the staff papers he had been using.
Diefenbaker not only expropriated the
paper but threatened to expose it publicly,
claiming that it referred to him as an s.o.b.
(Apparently this was a typically illegible
reference to the OAS (Organization of
American States), which the President was
urging Canada to join. 'I couldn't have
called him an s.o.b.,' commented Kennedy
later. 'I didn't know he was one — at that
time.')"
— *Theodore C. Sorensen*
Kennedy

**". . . that story was** a Liberal invention
designed to provide a context for the
Kennedy joke that he hadn't known I was
(an s.o.b.) until that meeting."
— *John Diefenbaker*
One Canada: Volume 2

*MACPHERSON*
*THE TORONTO STAR, MAY, 1961*

"**The only Canadian** in power who dared seriously to question the wisdom of American leadership in defence and foreign policy was John G. Diefenbaker. He declined to make the automatic response to American initiative in the Cuban crisis in the autumn of 1962; he dared to postpone the adoption of nuclear weapons for the Canadian Armed Forces against the wishes of the Kennedy administration; and, as a result, he was attacked by the Kennedy administration, as well as by the official Liberal Opposition in Canada, and defeated by the Canadian people in the election of 1963."

*— Donald Creighton*
Towards the Discovery of Canada

"**We shall be** Canadians first, foremost and always, and our policies will be decided in Canada and not dictated by any other country."

*— John Diefenbaker*
*Rimouski, Quebec, May 8, 1962*
*from* Quotations from Chairman Diefenbaker

*HUNTER*
*LE SOLEIL, DECEMBER, 1960*

**"I have an** intense hatred for
discrimination based on colour."
*— John Diefenbaker*
Maclean's *Magazine, March 29, 1958*
*from John Munro*
The Wit and Wisdom of John Diefenbaker

**"John Diefenbaker is** going to be
troublesome about South Africa. He is
taking a 'holier than thou' attitude, which
may cause us infinite trouble."
*— Harold Macmillan*
*then British Prime Minister*
*from* Memoirs: Pointing the Way, 1959-1961

*McNALLY*
*MONTREAL STAR, MARCH, 1961*

*"Dr. Verwoerd says Canada's attitude is immature."*

**"He was a** prophet who promised a brilliant future, an evangelist who offered redemption from an evil past, a prosecuting counsel determined on the conviction of a particularly notorious criminal."

— *Donald Creighton*
The Forked Road

**"Dear Sir:**

This is to inform you that some crackpot is using your name and has recently written to me over your signature putting forward views so eccentric in nature and so much at variance with your usual logical style that the letter could not possibly be from you. I felt I owed it to you to bring this to your attention."

— *John Diefenbaker*
*He would send this letter in reply*
*to letters received which displeased him.*
*from Thomas Van Dusen*
The Chief

**"And that was** the trouble: Lester Pearson was always being compared to John Diefenbaker, who was one of the greatest political campaigners in Canadian history, if not the greatest."

— *Peter Stursberg*
Lester Pearson and the Dream of Unity

**"In the personal** duel between a prime minister and an opposition leader, it is usually the opposition man who is cast in the role of tormenter.

But with John Diefenbaker and Lester Pearson it has been the other way around. Old trial lawyer Diefenbaker, more times than not, has been able to turn the tables of debate on old diplomat Pearson, leaving him in a state of head-clutching rage and frustration."

— *Charles Lynch*
*Southam Newspapers*
*January 20, 1960*

**"My test for** a political leader, or indeed any politician, is very simple. Is he honest and sincere, and is he a man of strong character who would never sacrifice his principles for office or for power?

"I reckon Diefenbaker stands up well to this test. He appears to me to grow in stature as the years go by."

— *Field-Marshall Viscount Montgomery*
The Toronto Telegram
*June 27, 1960*
*from the Diefenbaker scrapbook, June, 1960*

*MACPHERSON*
*THE TORONTO STAR, 1961*

**"The besetting disease** of Canadian public life for almost a decade has been Diefenbakerism: the belief that promises were policies, that rhetoric was action, and that the electorate believed in Santa Claus.''

*— Ramsey Cook*
*from John Robert Columbo*
Columbo's Canadian Quotations

**"Cuba was Diefenbaker's** watershed, beyond which his political fortunes were to flow sometimes sharply, and sometimes imperceptibly, but always irrevocably, downhill.''

*— Patrick Nicholson*
Vision and Indecision

*KUCH*
*WINNIPEG FREE PRESS, FEBRUARY 28, 1962*

*"Harvey and Friend"*

# Blandly

*This* Blondie *parody appeared in a 1962 newspaper parody called* The Montreal Stare. *The election was called April 18, 1962.*

*"Oh it's beginning to look like June, tra-la"*

*McNALLY*
*MONTREAL STAR, APRIL, 1962*

"**I understand (Pearson)** went across Canada taking a poll of what people want. Whatever they want, he's for. The Liberals are the flying saucers of politics. No one can make head or tail of them and they are never seen twice in the same place."
— *John Diefenbaker*
*London, Ontario, May 5, 1962*
*from* Quotations from Chairman Diefenbaker

"**I might have** had an easier life if he had been deposed a year or two earlier."
— *Lester B. Pearson*
Mike: Volume 3

"**Even a fish** would avoid trouble if he KEPT HIS MOUTH SHUT"
— *Sign on the desk of James Nelson,*
*Diefenbaker's press secretary*
*1960*

*MACPHERSON*
*THE TORONTO STAR, APRIL, 1962*

"I've Got a Secret"

"**I have always** thought of an election as a great trial in which the electorate listens to and weighs the evidence. I have found too, from my experience in previous elections, that a reasonable presentation of the facts must win the verdict."
— *John Diefenbaker*
*Television interview, June 14, 1962*
*from* Quotations from Chairman Diefenbaker

*COLLINS*
*MONTREAL GAZETTE, APRIL, 1962*

"Mother-in-law trouble"

*TING*
*LONDON FREE PRESS, JUNE, 1962*

**"I'm disturbed because** the doctors tell me
I'm as sound as a dollar.''
*— John Diefenbaker*
*House of Commons, April 25, 1975*

*KUCH*
*WINNIPEG FREE PRESS, MAY 2, 1962*

**"Prime Minister Diefenbaker** has decided to call his new dog 'Happy.' The name was selected from thousands of suggestions the Prime Minister received since his wife gave him the dog as a Christmas present."

— The Montreal Gazette
*January 11, 1962*

*Practical joke prepared by the Ottawa Press Gallery from the Diefenbaker scrapbook, February, 1962*

*"Grrr . . ."*

*BEATON*
*TORONTO TELEGRAM, MAY 18, 1962*

**"I think that** he got to the place where he thought that everybody was 'agin im.' "
— *Ellen Fairclough on the aftermath of the*
*1962 election*
*quoted in* Diefenbaker: Leadership Lost

**"As I listen** to my honourable friend, I think of those words in the scriptures:
'Paul, thou art beside thyself! Much learning doth make thee mad.' "
— *John Diefenbaker*
*House of Commons, October 2, 1962*
*(after being interrupted repeatedly*
*by Paul Martin)*
*from* Quotations from Chairman Diefenbaker

**"The party fell** apart. The ministers resigned, the leader was being slowly murdered by his ministers; they destroyed the party themselves."
— *Pierre Elliott Trudeau*
*Ottawa, Ontario, September, 1973*

**"Diefenbaker's government had** inherited far worse problems from the Liberals than it or most Canadians realized and its huge majority left it no alibis."
— *Desmond Morton*
A Short History of Canada

*MACPHERSON*
*THE TORONTO STAR, FEBRUARY 5, 1963*

*"What happened to my strawberries?"*

"**I never saw** such an example of political courage as John Diefenbaker's, fighting that election entirely on his own. Imagine that man, with his Cabinet in ruins about him; yet he fought the election through literally by himself, made a very respectable showing, and won many more seats than anyone had expected."

*— Harold Macmillan*
*British Prime Minister in 1963*
*from Patrick Nicholson*
Vision and Indecision

*MACPHERSON*
*THE TORONTO STAR, MARCH 12, 1963*

"**I know there** are powerful interests against me. They were against me in 1956 and are again today."

— *John Diefenbaker*
*Port Hope, Ontario, March 8, 1963*
*from* Quotations from Chairman Diefenbaker

"**Everyone is against** me — except the people."

— *John Diefenbaker*
*(slogan used in 1963 election campaign)*

"**I told Diefenbaker** about what issues I thought were hurting most — lack of attention to housing and to urban issues generally. The impression in my riding was that if a western wheat farmer sneezed, half the bloody cabinet would get on a plane with a box of Kleenex and head out to look after it. This was almost today's western disorientation in reverse."

— *Frank McGee on the 1962 election*
*quoted in* Diefenbaker: Leadership Lost

"**Eugene Forsey believed** that the verdict of history might 'very well be that the Diefenbaker government did a lot of awfully good work, solid work, and helped to get the country through a very difficult period with a reasonable degree of success.' His assessment of Diefenbaker was that he was a much better prime minister than most people gave him credit for being."

— *Peter Stursberg*
Diefenbaker: Leadership Lost

*"February the fifth and all's not well!"*

*FRANKLIN*
*THE GLOBE AND MAIL, FEBRUARY 6, 1963*

DIEFENBAKER: Remembering the Chief

"**So an easy** victim was chosen; the command was given: Diefenbaker must go!"

*— Pierre Trudeau accusing the John F. Kennedy administration of conspiring to get rid of Diefenbaker, in a 1963* Cité Libre *article*

"**As far as** the (Cuban) missile crisis itself was concerned, I thought Diefenbaker handled that not too badly at all. . . His annoyance with Washington for not being informed was perfectly justified. It was an expression of Diefenbaker's lifelong, instinctive Canadianism. . . All my colleagues were with him. Certainly I was. I objected as strongly as he appeared to do to just saying 'aye' because Washington wanted something done. . . I thought he handled that as a Canadian would."

*— David Lewis quoted in* Diefenbaker: Leadership Lost

"**I don't need** a Beatle haircut. With what the cartoonists can do with my hair, I need no assistance."

*— John Diefenbaker Fredericton, N.B., September 11, 1964 from* Quotations from Chairman Diefenbaker

"**The 1963 election** returned the Liberals to power, but John Diefenbaker, travelling the country by train, almost won the election for his party. It was possibly the greatest, most spectacular one-man political campaign in Canadian history."

*— from a brochure published by the Right Honourable John G. Diefenbaker Centre, Saskatoon, Saskatchewan.*

"**My main political** asset is that I know what Canadians are thinking."

*— John Diefenbaker Television interview, April 4, 1963 from* Quotations from Chairman Diefenbaker

"**I don't campaign.** I just visit with the people."

*— John Diefenbaker Campaign Picnic, 1965 from* Quotations from Chairman Diefenbaker

*GAGNIER LE DEVOIR (MONTREAL), FEBRUARY 9, 1963*

*"Les Américains m'ont joué dans les cheveaux!" / "The Americans have been playing in my hair!"*

# "THROW THE RASCALS IN"

## The Opposition Years

*"If he says he's the Leader of the Opposition, humor him."*

MACPHERSON
*THE TORONTO STAR, JULY 28, 1964*

"**Oppositions cleanse and** purify those
in office and we in the opposition are in fact
the 'detergents of democracy.' "
*— John Diefenbaker*
*House of Commons*
*November 24, 1964*

"**(Being in opposition)** is where he's at
his best, because he is the master
interrogator, the Prince Rupert of the
cavalry attack. He is superb at this, and he
is a good parliamentarian. Consequently, as
a leader of the opposition he is most
effective, much more effective than he is in
government."
*— Tommy Douglas*
*quoted in* Diefenbaker: Leadership Lost

"**I've enjoyed my** two periods as leader
of the opposition. It's a much freer life than
Prime Minister and you have an almost
equal scope of making a contribution."
*— John Diefenbaker*
*Ottawa, September 18, 1964*
*from* Quotations from Chairman Diefenbaker

"**They think I'm** fighting too hard. I
don't know any other way to fight."
*— John Diefenbaker in opposition 1965*

*MACPHERSON*
*THE TORONTO STAR, 1963*

"**John Diefenbaker enjoyed** and often told the story of a southern Baptist minister explaining his success as a preacher: 'First I tells them what my message is going to be; next, I tells them my message; then, I tells them what my message was.' "

— *John Munro*
The Wit and Wisdom of John Diefenbaker

"**It has been** said of me that when I speak I always have three speeches: the one I intend to make, the one I give to the press that I don't use, and the one I finally deliver to the audience. It is amazing what audiences can do for a speaker . . . to read a prepared text is to miss it all."

— *John Diefenbaker*
One Canada: Volume 2

"**Oh, I've got** a new Macdonald story. John A. was on a public platform with a Temperance person. And he said to the Temperance man, 'Would you move away please, your breath smells terrible . . . It smells of water.' "

— *John Diefenbaker*
*from* Quotations from Chairman Diefenbaker
*(Diefenbaker was in fact a teetotaler most of his life)*

*MACPHERSON*
*THE TORONTO STAR, APRIL 6, 1964*

*"Five minutes before House is in session, Mr. Diefenbaker."*

*NORRIS*
*VANCOUVER SUN, MAY 20, 1964*

**"Does it move** your heart to see this flag after it has flown for a week or ten days? Does it touch you as freedom's banner streaming o'er us? Does it consecrate in everyone looking at it the history, the struggle, the strife that brought about our Canada? Sir, a flag cannot be created by one man, however powerful his position. This is a time of instant creation but you cannot create instant flags. Flags are born in the strife and turmoil of the clash of history. They are not the result of an egocentric decision.''

— *John Diefenbaker*
*House of Commons*
*September 1, 1964*

*BLAINE*
*THE HAMILTON SPECTATOR, JULY, 1964*

"A simple 'Yes' or 'No' will suffice."

MACPHERSON
THE TORONTO STAR, OCTOBER 30, 1964

**"I ask you,** how far are you going to be able to see that white flag in winter?"
— *John Diefenbaker*
*House of Commons*
*June 15, 1964*

**"Contrary to some** stories from Ottawa, there was never any problem in our personal relations. . . Mr. Diefenbaker was always amiable and of good value. . . his story-telling and anecdotal abilities were famous."

— *Lester B. Pearson*
Mike: Volume 3

*TING*
*LONDON FREE PRESS, DECEMBER, 1964*

*"Well, I've gotta admit it is distinctive."*

"**Parliament is a** place honored by
tradition and hallowed by the greatness of
its history."

*— John Diefenbaker*
One Canada: Volume 2

*MACPHERSON
THE TORONTO STAR, JANUARY 19, 1966*

*''Then KAPOW! I'll flatten the opposition!''*

**"I have often** thought of my honourable friend, the Minister of Citizenship and Immigration (J.W. Pickersgill) as a "Gliberal." He would believe anything twice, as Mencken once said."
— *John Diefenbaker*
*House of Commons*
*April 12, 1956*

**(A suggested campaign** slogan for the scandal-ridden Liberals):
"Throw the rascals in."
— *John Diefenbaker*
*1965 election campaign*
*from Margaret Wente*
I Never Say Anything Provocative

**"Never in Canadian** history has there been a government so prone to be prone."
— *John Diefenbaker*
*House of Commons*
*January 20, 1966*

*BEATON*
*TORONTO TELEGRAM, MARCH 8, 1966*

*"I'll call your security bet and raise you a sex scandal . . ."*

# "I'LL RISE AND FIGHT AGAIN"

## Leadership Lost

*"What time's the funeral? I wouldn't want to miss it."*

*TING*
*LONDON FREE PRESS*

**"The Old Chief** must have wondered why so many Conservatives turned against his assertive leadership at a time when the weakness and confusion of the Liberal Government invited defeat. The trouble was that instead of measuring him against the political frailties of Lester Pearson, his one-time disciples were remembering with a sense of profound disillusion the inspired Diefenbaker they had followed out of the political wilderness in 1957 and 1958. By the mid-sixties, his vision of Canada, once so relevant to their demands, no longer fitted into the mainstream of responsible Conservative thought.

"Like many another political hero, John Diefenbaker was frozen in history at the moment of his triumph. His great electoral victories condemned him to a permanent sense of anti-climax."

— *Peter C. Newman*
Distemper of our Times

*TING*
*LONDON FREE PRESS, SEPTEMBER, 1967*

*"Hippity Hoppin' Down the Rumor Trail"*

"**(The meeting of** the officers of the national executive of the Conservative Party) was scheduled to open with a speech by Léon Balcer, leader of the rebels (opposed to Diefenbaker's continuing leadership.)

"Only a few feet away from him sat Diefenbaker. In the face of his chief, Balcer ducked the moment of truth. Instead of delivering a fighting speech on the wrongs he considered Diefenbaker had done to French Canada, Balcer said quietly, 'My views are well known,' and sat down.

"During the long, astonished silence which followed, one delegate expostulated: 'That's great. That really changes my opinion.' "

— *Richard Gwyn*
The Shape of Scandal

*MACPHERSON*
*THE TORONTO STAR, MARCH 8, 1966*

*"John G. Diefenbaker speaking."*

*BLAINE*
*THE HAMILTON SPECTATOR, NOVEMBER, 1966*

"**The papers say** Dalton Camp is
revolting. I cannot disagree."
— *John Diefenbaker*
*from Carolyn Weir*
Diefenbaker: A Pictorial Tribute

*RUSINS*
*OTTAWA CITIZEN, AUGUST, 1967*

**"The 'termites' — as** Diefenbaker called them — vented their frustration with increasing bitterness and decreasing hope as the months and years dragged on."

— *Geoffrey Stevens*
Stanfield

**"From November (1965)** until May (1966), the Conservative chieftains waited to hear his resignation, like officers in a Prussian regimental mess anticipating the shot that would tell them their disgraced colonel had taken the gentlemanly way out. It never came. And slowly, reluctantly, the dread machinery of court martial was set into motion."

— *Martin Sullivan*
Mandate '68

**"When John Diefenbaker** enters a room, I stand up."

— *Arthur Maloney*
*Progressive Conservative Annual Meeting*
*November, 1966*

*BEATON*
*TORONTO TELEGRAM, SEPTEMBER 26, 1966*

*"Step into my other office . . . ."*

"**The execution of** John Diefenbaker."
— *from Geoffrey Stevens*
Stanfield
*(in reference to the 1967 leadership*
*convention)*

"**Fight on, my** men . . .
I am wounded but I am not slain
I'll lay me down and bleed awhile
and then I'll rise and fight again"
— *Diefenbaker quoted from this poem by Sir*
*Andrew Barton, an Elizabethan soldier,*
*when, on November 16, 1966, the*
*Conservative party decided to hold a*
*leadership convention.*
One Canada: Volume 3

"**I was wounded,** but I was not slain. I
will stop and I will rest, and I will start
again."
— *Jean Chrétien, after losing the Liberal*
*leadership to John Turner, June, 1984.*
*From an article by Roy MacGregor,*
Toronto Sunday Star, *August 19, 1984.*
*Neither Chrétien nor MacGregor*
*acknowledged a debt to either*
*Diefenbaker or Barton.*

*MACPHERSON*
*THE TORONTO STAR, NOVEMBER 17, 1966*

*"But Mr. Camp, what will you do for an encore?"*

*The Saga of John Diefenbaker and His Mutinous Crew''*

*MACPHERSON*
*THE TORONTO STAR, MAY 30, 1967*

"**Many wished that** John George Diefenbaker had passed into political history long before the convention opened. But in the nine days that crowded upon one another that September, the old Chief was to be the conscience of the party that had tried to forget him, and the defender of the Canadian nation which he loved and never forgot."

— *James Johnston*
The Party's Over

"*If there's any thinking to be done around here, I'll do it!*"

CHAMBERS
*HALIFAX CHRONICLE HERALD, AUGUST 8, 1967*

**"A rewarding moment** occurred when John Bracken, former Conservative leader, appeared at Diefenbaker's side in the Gardens box, recalling Diefenbaker's defence of Bracken's leadership in the face of caucus determination to dump Bracken in 1947. Diefenbaker's defence had not prevailed, but Bracken had not forgotten.''
— *Thomas Van Dusen*
*The Chief*
*(describing the 1967 convention)*

**"They criticized me** sometimes for being too much concerned with the average Canadian. I can't help that. I'm just one of them.''
— *John Diefenbaker*
*Toronto, Ontario, September 7, 1967*

**"We weren't always** right. One time an Ontario leader came up to Macdonald and he said, 'You know, Sir John, I'm always with you when you're right.' Sir John told him where he might go. 'What I need is people who are with me when we're wrong.' ''
— *John Diefenbaker*
*Toronto, Ontario, September 7, 1967*

**"I am asked** — and I am speaking to young Canada now — are there any rewards in public life? There are — not monetary, but there is a tremendous satisfaction in being able to say, 'I tried, I stood.' ''
— *John Diefenbaker*
*Leadership convention in Toronto*
*September 9, 1967*

**"My course has** come to an end. I have fought your battles, and you have given me loyalty that led us to victory more often than the party ever had since the days of John A. Macdonald. In my retiring I have nothing to withdraw in my desire to see Canada, my country and your country, one nation.''
— *John Diefenbaker*
*Progressive Conservative*
*Leadership Convention*
*Toronto, Ontario, September 9, 1967*

**"So I think** Diefenbaker's fight was successful. He was able to get the ('two nations') resolution withdrawn entirely and it never became official policy. I would think that he has the perfect right to claim that he stopped the Conservative party from making a grievous error.''
— *Alvin Hamilton*
*quoted in* Diefenbaker: Leadership Lost

**"(After withdrawing from** the leadership contest) the Chief was completely relaxed. He was a new man. It's just as if a great burden had been lifted off him. We were rather depressed and hot and tired, and all of a sudden this strange, reedy tenor split the silence. It was the Chief, singing 'When You Come to the End of a Perfect Day.' It was a very appropriate piece, but it was a very poor rendition.''
— *Greg Guthrie*
*Diefenbaker's 'special assistant, bodyguard,*
*and second'*
*quoted in* Diefenbaker: Leadership Lost

*McNALLY*
*MONTREAL STAR, SEPTEMBER, 1967*

*''Is this where the love-in is being held?''*

# "WELL, THE DOCTORS ARE ALL GONE"

## The Saga Continues

*FRANKLIN*
*THE GLOBE AND MAIL, MARCH, 1970*

**"In 1916 overseas** I was injured accidentally and it was said that I did not have long to live.

"Well, the doctors are all gone."
*— John Diefenbaker*
*Hamilton, Ontario, June 19, 1974*

**"The Prime Minister** announced a war on poverty. I was impressed. He appointed Tom Kent to run his war on poverty. . . that was impressive too. And they raised Kent's salary from $12,000 a year to $25,000. . . He won *his* war on poverty."
*— John Diefenbaker*
*Oakville, Ontario, September 18, 1965*
*from* Quotations from Chairman Diefenbaker

**"I just speak** the truth, and as someone once said, interrupting me in an audience, 'Give 'em hell, John.' And I said, 'I never do that. I just tell the truth and it sounds like hell.' "
*— John Diefenbaker*
*(a story recounted on many occasions)*

**"John Diefenbaker is** dead, but his spirit lives on in this election campaign.

"Progressive Conservative leader Brian Mulroney has resurrected Dief's old 'One Canada' line, coined in the 50s, and he is fond of saying in campaign speeches that 'I don't give them hell — I just tell the truth and it sounds like hell.' "
— Toronto Star
*August 5, 1984*

*MACPHERSON*
*THE TORONTO STAR, SEPTEMBER 3, 1969*

"Quasimodo"

"**Diefenbaker was — and** is — a larger figure than any Canadian Tory leader since Macdonald, and he will stand in history among the grandiose failures who in Canada are always so much more appealing than those who succeed; men like Louis Riel and Henri Bourassa and the attractive but doomed leader of French-Canadian separatism, René Lévesque. But, for all his oratorical spellbinding and his talent for political guerilla warfare, Diefenbaker belonged to an age that was already past in Canada. He was — in spite of the Conservative label — the last of the great prairie radicals, trying to impose the values of the Deep West on a society that was already urban and industrial. . ."

— *George Woodcock*
Canada and the Canadians

*MACPHERSON*
*THE TORONTO STAR, MAY 29, 1968*

*''Looks like it's going to be another one of those days.''*

**"He wasn't always** right! Sometimes he was on the wrong side, but never on the side of wrong!''
  — *Diefenbaker often hoped that this would be said of him, as it was said of "another in public service."*

**"I thought Diefenbaker** must have been a great defence lawyer, although he was a great parliamentarian. I mean the guy made the greatest speeches I ever heard in the House of Commons and that was when he was past his prime. But I tell you, he was sensational.
  ''The only man who could approach him, in my view, was Tommy Douglas, and Allan MacEachen at his best could be pretty good. But Dief really could be electrifying. His phrases were evocative.''
                — *John Turner*
                *from Jack Cahill*
       John Turner: The Long Run

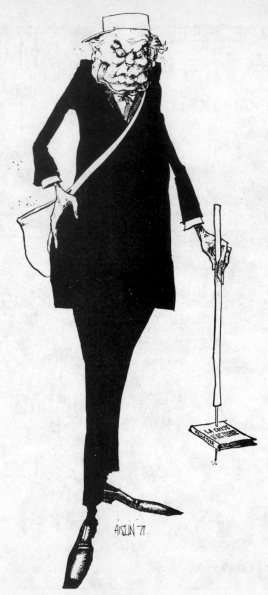

*AISLIN*
*MONTREAL STAR, 1971*

*"John Diefenbaker court après sa proie."* / *"John Diefenbaker on the prowl."*

BLAINE
THE HAMILTON SPECTATOR, 1971

"**I can assure** you that as long as there is a drop of blood in my body, they won't stop me from talking about freedom."
— *John Diefenbaker*
*Sudbury, Ontario, June 3, 1962*
*from* Quotations from Chairman Diefenbaker

DOWN WITH CREEPING REPUBLICANISM.!!

*AISLIN*
*MONTREAL GAZETTE, 1972*

**"The Chancellor** (of the University of Punjab, India) said that I was a graduate of the University of Saskatchewan. The word 'Saskatchewan' gave him some difficulty. In my response I told the story of two English ladies who were crossing Canada by train. At Saskatoon, where there was a brief stop, one of the ladies asked a man standing on a platform the name of the city. When he replied 'Saskatoon, Saskatchewan,' she commented to her companion, 'Well, it's obvious they don't speak English here.' "

— *John Diefenbaker from Carolyn Weir*
Diefenbaker: A Pictorial Tribute

**"(Sir Wilfred Laurier's)** private railway car was at the (Saskatoon) station one morning when I went over to pick up our newspapers. There he was, standing on the platform, taking the morning air. This memory of him will stay with me always, his dignity, his plume of snow-white hair. I sold him a newspaper. He gave me a quarter — no better way to establish an instant rapport with a newsboy. We chatted about Canada. I had the awed feeling that I was in the presence of greatness. That afternoon, when he laid the cornerstone (of the University of Saskatchewan), he included in his remarks a reference to his conversation with a Saskatoon newsboy, which, he observed, had ended with my saying, 'Sorry, Prime Minister, I can't waste any more time on you, I've got work to do.' "

— *John Diefenbaker*
One Canada: Volume 1

GORDIE HOWE IS ALSO FROM SASKATCHEWAN !!

GORDIE HOWE EST UN AUTRE VIEUX CHEVAL DE LA SASKATCHEWAN!

*AISLIN*
*MONTREAL GAZETTE, 1974*

**"Bastards I Have** Known"
*— John Diefenbaker kidded reporters that
this was to be the title of the fourth
volume of his memoirs.*
*from John Munro*
The Wit and Wisdom of John Diefenbaker

**"The bouncing Czech."**
*— John Diefenbaker referring to
Peter C. Newman*

**"What determines the** character of a
man? Whence does he get his strength to
endure, to abide by his principles, and to
reject the concept of the impossible in
human affairs? It is my conviction that a
man is the end product of his ancestors,
proximate and remote, that he is endowed
at birth with a heritage of character, but
that this character may be influenced by
fortuitous circumstances."
*— John Diefenbaker*
*Opening paragraph of*
One Canada: Volume 1

*AISLIN*
*MONTREAL GAZETTE, 1975*

*"The Diefenbaker memoirs"*

# "A CELEBRATION OF A LIFE WELL LIVED"

## The Final Years

*RUSINS*
*OTTAWA CITIZEN, SEPTEMBER 18, 1975*

"**When somebody dies** at the age of 83, it isn't a time for sadness. It is time for a celebration of a life well lived."
— *Stanley Knowles*
*August 16, 1979*

"**When John Diefenbaker** was visiting me in London in the 1970s to receive the Companion of Honour from Queen Elizabeth II, he referred to the Companion of the Order of Canada as the 'Cuckoo' award, compared to his C.H. A reporter overheard his comment and exclaimed, 'Oh, Mr. Diefenbaker! How can you say that when Paul Martin received that recognition only a few days ago?' Thinking quickly, Diefenbaker restored, '*He* is the only one to have deserved it.''
— *Paul Martin*
Far From Home

"**My country has** been good to me. I'm glad that I have lived in this age."
— *John Diefenbaker*
*from* Quotations from Chairman Diefenbaker

"**God has been** good to me. Mine has been a long life and I feel privileged to have had the opportunity to continue serving Canada in the House of Commons. The Canadian people, without regard to political affiliation, have given me their affection. I bear no ill-feeling to those who, in the past, opposed me. But I stand today, as I have always stood, for principle:
Freedom and Equality for all Canadians, however humble their lot in life and whatever their racial origin. One Canada, One Nation''
— *John Diefenbaker*
One Canada: Volume 3
*(the conclusion of his memoirs)*

"**Nothing I ever** do is political."
— *John Diefenbaker*
*Ottawa, January 16, 1978*
*from* Quotations from Chairman Diefenbaker

*RUSINS*
*OTTAWA CITIZEN, FEBRUARY, 1976*

*MACPHERSON*
*THE TORONTO STAR, OCTOBER 22, 1976*

*DONATO*
*THE TORONTO SUN, 1979*

**Right Hon. J.G.** Diefenbaker (Prince Albert): Mr. Speaker, I rise, under the provisions of Standing Order 43, on an important matter on this historic date for all mankind. I move, on behalf of Canada whose devotion to peace has been proven over and over, seconded by the Secretary of State for External Affairs (Mr. Jamieson), the following:

That this House expresses its deep appreciation to President Carter, to the Prime Minister of Israel and to the President of Egypt at having been successful in producing a treaty which this House had hoped for as expressed in a resolution on March 7, and, furthermore, as the heads of these two countries have received the Nobel Peace Prize, and as each of them has spoken warmly of President Carter's contribution, that an award of the Nobel Peace Prize to him would be welcomed not only by Canadians but by peace-loving people of all mankind.

(After several people spoke in favour of the motion:)

Mr. Speaker: The House has heard the terms of the motion moved by Mr. Diefenbaker and seconded by Mr. Jamieson.

Is it the pleasure of the House to adopt the said motion?

Motion agreed to.

Mr. Speaker: The House will, I am sure, want to observe that there could scarcely be a more fitting way to celebrate the thirty-ninth anniversary of the right hon. gentleman's election to parliament which is being celebrated today.

Some Hon. Members: Hear, hear!

*— John Diefenbaker's last speech in the*
*House of Commons*
*March 26, 1979*

"**I can say** this. That there is nothing more lonely than being a former Prime Minister of Canada and the only one. And I join with you in the prophecy that next Tuesday night, I'll have company."
— *John Diefenbaker*
*The Last Rally*
*Prince Albert, Sask., May 15, 1979*
*He was right, of course, and on May 22*
*Pierre Elliott Trudeau was able to*
*double the ranks of the 'Former Prime*
*Minister's Club.'*

*AISLIN*
*MONTREAL GAZETTE, MARCH 6, 1979*

NEWS ITEM: DIEFENBAKER IS PREPARING FOR ELECTION.

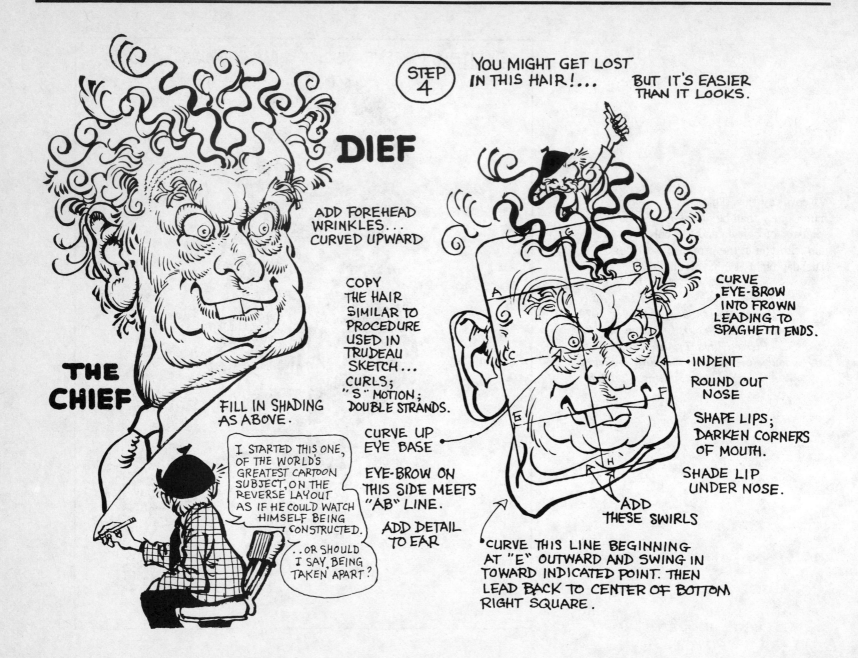

STEP 4

YOU MIGHT GET LOST IN THIS HAIR!... BUT IT'S EASIER THAN IT LOOKS.

DIEF

THE CHIEF

ADD FOREHEAD WRINKLES... CURVED UPWARD

COPY THE HAIR SIMILAR TO PROCEDURE USED IN TRUDEAU SKETCH... CURLS; "S" MOTION; DOUBLE STRANDS.

CURVE EYE-BROW INTO FROWN LEADING TO SPAGHETTI ENDS.

INDENT
ROUND OUT NOSE

SHAPE LIPS; DARKEN CORNERS OF MOUTH.

SHADE LIP UNDER NOSE.

FILL IN SHADING AS ABOVE.

CURVE UP EYE BASE

EYE-BROW ON THIS SIDE MEETS "AB" LINE.

ADD DETAIL TO EAR

ADD THESE SWIRLS

CURVE THIS LINE BEGINNING AT "E" OUTWARD AND SWING IN TOWARD INDICATED POINT. THEN LEAD BACK TO CENTER OF BOTTOM RIGHT SQUARE.

I STARTED THIS ONE, OF THE WORLD'S GREATEST CARTOON SUBJECT, ON THE REVERSE LAYOUT AS IF HE COULD WATCH HIMSELF BEING CONSTRUCTED.

..OR SHOULD I SAY, BEING TAKEN APART?

138

③ DRAW NOSTRIL AT DOTTED LINE WHICH IS HALF-WAY MARK OF THAT SECTION, BETWEEN THE TWO STARS ✳. THE LOWER NOSE IS SHAPED LIKE A "G" AND A "W" COMBINED. COPY AS SHOWN ENDING NEXT TO LEFT EYE.

JOIN BOTH EYES WITH FROWN REPRESENTED BY A LARGE "W"

② DIVIDE IT IN HALF, BOTH WAYS AND IN QUARTERS — TOP TO BOTTOM.

PLACE TWO CIRCLES ON HALF-WAY MARK "CD"... THE LEFT CIRCLE BIGGER THAN THE RIGHT... DRAW EYE CENTERS INSIDE IN POSITIONS SHOWN.

① FIRST DRAW A RECTANGLE: TO CUT IN HALVES OR QUARTERS MARK THE EDGE OF A PAPER AND MEASURE AGAINST OTHER PART.

½ LONGER THAN IT IS WIDE

BEGIN EAR JUST BELOW "A"

AND JUST ABOVE "E". EAR LOOKS LIKE HANDLE ON A MUG

SMILE

COPY CLOUD-LIKE CHIN.

DRAW CURVES ABOVE BOTH EYES FOR LIDS... PLUS ((( SHADING UNDER EYES FORMING "SUITCASES"

NOTICE: LEFT EYE IS IN LINE WITH POSITION FOR CORNER OF MOUTH. COPY TEETH AT INTERSECTION OF "EF" AND "GH".

THE BETTER YOU JUDGE THESE DISTANCES ⌐ THE BETTER YOUR FINISHED PRODUCT... YOU DON'T HAVE TO BE TOO EXACT THOUGH.

ONE-WAY

SMILE

©1971 Blaine

BLAINE
THE HAMILTON SPECTATOR, 1971

**"He was the** best there is. He's going to be missed by a lot of cartoonists, I can tell you that.

"We always loved it when he was in the news. He was such a character and such a delight to draw. He was a jovial, witty guy — a walking cartoon.

"He was bright, really a brilliant guy. Right up to the end, he had a brain that was really on."

— *Blaine*
*Hamilton Spectator editorial cartoonist*
The Hamilton Spectator
*August 16, 1979*

*This is an envelope in which Blaine sent a cartoon to Diefenbaker. Note that the only part of the name and address given is "Ottawa, Canada." The date on the envelope is July 12, 1965.*

FROM: Blaine (EDITORIAL CARTOONIST),
THE HAMILTON SPECTATOR

"**If it were** up to the cartoonists, Mr. Diefenbaker would remain Prime Minister by acclamation. He's our delight."
— *Al Beaton*
*Toronto Telegram editorial cartoonist*
The Toronto Telegram
*April 24, 1962*

"**I have been** caricatured thousands of times, and I doubt if anyone enjoys these things more that I do; if one cannot laugh at oneself, there is little hope of survival in political life."
— *John Diefenbaker*
One Canada: Volume 3

"**I think cartoons** serve a very useful purpose. I see all the cartoons. Macdonald used to say he had the ugliest face of anyone of his time, but if Macdonald could see the cartoons today, he would conclude that he's in second place."
— *John Diefenbaker*
The Star Weekly
*September 2, 1967*
*from* Quotations from Chairman Diefenbaker

"**Careful you don't** overdo this. I don't want people to say a great transformation has taken place. The caricaturists won't have any subject matter anymore."
— *John Diefenbaker in a TV make-up room*
*Toronto, Ontario, October 3, 1965*
*from* Quotations from Chairman Diefenbaker

"**Prime Minister John** Diefenbaker has a wall full of cartoons in the recreation room of his house. They're not all flattering, by any means, but that doesn't seem to worry him."
— *Charles Nichols*
The Toronto Telegram
*April 24, 1962*

"**Canada's Prime Minister** was accorded the praise of Britain's top political cartoonist in Montreal yesterday. But the praise was in terms best understood by a cartoonist.

"David Low (creator of 'Colonel Blimp') looks upon John Diefenbaker as a bright light in a world of otherwise dim cartoon subjects.

" 'Canadian cartoonists are fortunate to have him,' he said. 'To me, he suggests a parrot or perhaps a cockatoo. Actually, his face is full of suggestion.' "
— *an article in the* Montreal Gazette
*May 10, 1958*
*from the Diefenbaker scrapbook, May, 1958*

*TING*
*LONDON FREE PRESS*

**JOHN**
**Oh, don't go** yet. I'm going to have a wee dram.

EDNA
Oh, maybe I'll have one too.

JOHN (pouring brandy for both)
Two tries for the leadership. '42 and '48. I think I'll try again in '54. I'll make it a six year event: 'Diefenbaker tries for the Conservative leadership, it must be 1960!' Or maybe I'll just quit politics altogether.

EDNA
That's a good one.

JOHN
I wish you'd been with me when I went to Drew's suite to congratulate him. They were celebrating his victory, everybody toasting the new leader, when I walked in. *(Wrinkles his nose to indicate a bad smell.)* It was as if a black and white animal of the sort not customarily admitted to human company had suddenly entered the place.

EDNA
You'd think they were used to skunks in that menage.

JOHN
The more they dislike me, the more certain I am that I'm on the right track. John A. Macdonald used to say that his formula for success was a simple equation: let the number of your enemies be equal to the number of your friends.

EDNA
You haven't any trouble there.

JOHN
Not if you can keep the numbers up on the friends side! I'm quite good with the other.

— *from* Diefenbaker, *a play by*
*Thelma Oliver*
*first produced, October, 1983*

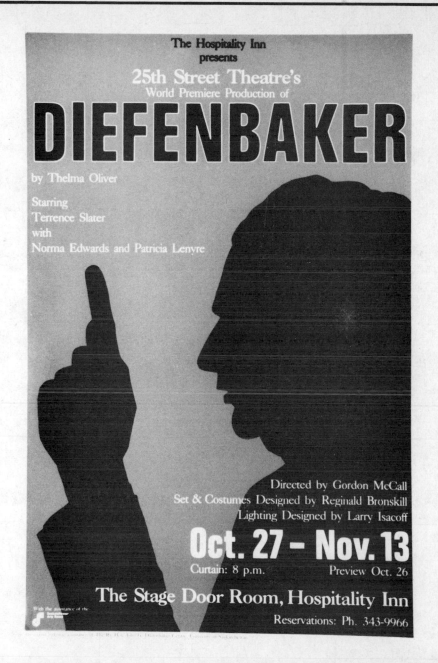

*SHELLY SOPHER*

# "DIEF IS THE CHIEF"

*ROSCHKOV*
*THE TORONTO STAR, AUGUST 17, 1979*

"**Dief is the** Chief, Dief is the Chief,
And Dief will be the Chief again.
Everybody's happy back in '57
And nobody's happy since then.
There was law in the land, order in the home.
Swimming in the river back then,
And I know in my heart that Dief will be the Chief
And a dollar worth a dollar again."
— *Bob Bossin, Stringband*
*"Dief Will Be the Chief Again"*

RUSINS
THE OTTAWA CITIZEN, FEBRUARY, 1976

"**Mr. Speaker, I** think it would be appropriate at this point in the proceedings of the first session of the Thirty-First Parliament for the House of Commons of Canada to pause and pay tribute to a man whose presence dominated this chamber for almost four decades, the late Right Honourable John George Diefenbaker . . .

"He was an indomitable man, a man of passion with strongly held and vigorously defended views, an unequivocal patriot whose commitment and devotion to Canada were beyond question, a statesman whose stature was enhanced by his warmth and by his personal approach toward the people and the land he loved so deeply. He was a singular man who entered and enlarged the lives of all of us as no one ever will again. Our people and our Parliament will miss him deeply."

— *Joe Clark addressing Parliament on the first day it reconvened after John Diefenbaker's death October 9, 1979*

"**I do not** know about other members, but I have the uneasy feeling he is still part of this place. Just this morning as I was speaking my thoughts on the role of the opposition when we elected you, Mr. Speaker, I half looked over at the other side expecting to see him shaking his finger at me and thundering, 'Never has there been such a conversion since Saul on the road to Damascus.'

"He sometimes mentioned to me the loneliness of being the only surviving former prime minister and seemed sincerely keen to have some company. I now know how he felt and sincerely share his keenness.

"It is sad that Mr. Diefenbaker is not here today, Mr. Speaker, and we shall miss him. But just speaking of the impact he made on Canadians and upon this House is a happy tribute to a person who knew the joy and satisfaction of doing what he wanted to do with his life and doing it to the best of his ability. What more could any of us wish as a record of our own ambitions and achievements?"

— *Pierre Trudeau on his first day in Parliament as leader of the opposition, continuing the eulogy*

". . . It is also important for those of us who are here and who hope to remain to note that at the same time he was an extraordinary populist in the sense that he never forgot that in a democracy it is essential to maintain the closest possible rapport with the ordinary citizen. He did not forget this at any point in his political life. He was also a notable, tough-minded fighter both against his enemies on the other side of the House and, from time to time, as his colleagues will recall, within his own party, when he thought a battle was in order. This, too, is something all of us in political life can learn from the memory of John Diefenbaker — that he fought for what he believed in. . ."

— *Ed Broadbent continuing the eulogy*

"**I had the** pleasure of meeting him in Quebec City on one of his visits there as a member of Parliament . . . I was curious to meet this fellow, if I may use this expression with reference to him, who had a bad reputation in the province of Quebec. He was reported to be hostile to French Canadians. Later on, after getting acquainted with his views and his intentions, I soon realized that this Canadian loved his country, every part of his country."

— *Adrian Lambert speaking on behalf of the Social Credit party (Creditistes)*

*DONATO*
*THE TORONTO SUN*

"**Still guiding us!**"

> *T.M., Vancouver, B.C.*

"**We need another** J.D."

> *M.H., Calgary, Alta.*

"**Nice to see** the Chief again"

> *A.R., Lambeth, Ont.*

"**We'll never find** another Dief"

> *J.E., Saskatoon, Sask.*

"**If only he** could have been immortal, we'd all be better off!"

> *T.W. & A.W., Alameda, Sask.*

"**Love that Dief**"

> *L. & J. O'H., Burnaby, B.C.*

"**Where's Dief — when** we need him!"

> *H.L., London, Ont.*

> *— comments in the guestbook from visitors to the Diefenbaker Centre, University of Saskatchewan, Saskatoon, Sask.*

*DONATO*
*THE TORONTO SUN, DECEMBER, 1979*

*"Loyalty is the great virtue for political leaders"*

Why did so many Canadians love John Diefenbaker? Watching his funeral on television, I had to ask myself why I should feel such affection for him, such a sense of debt for what he represented.

The trust of his countrymen had enabled him to break the long smooth reign of the Liberals from 1935-1957, and had been the basis of the enormous electoral victory of 1958. But this love was even more marked in the elections of 1963 and 1965. In those elections he had the full weight of the powerful classes against him (including its members in his own party) and was still able almost single-handed to prevent the Liberals from forming majority governments. This was probably his most remarkable political achievement, and certainly a mark of the affection he could summon forth.

This affection was not something shared by the clever or the rich or the slick of our society. When he was in power they feared him because he might take Canada off the smooth course they had charted since 1935, when he was out of office they despised him as a silly survivor from a well-forgotten past who did not know the score.

A young scion of great wealth in English-speaking Montreal said in 1965: "Oh George, how can you support such a vulgarian? Pearson is such a gentleman compared to that yahoo." The remark illustrated what the definition of gentleman had become in our society.

Of course, there was something in what the rich and the clever said about Diefenbaker. His rhetoric was indeed antediluvian; his egocentricity often seemed to transcend his principles. He often sounded the note of messianism without content. Above all his appalling choice of French colleagues suggested that he did not know the first principle of Canadian politics: no party can properly rule in Canada for long without solid support in Quebec. Why then did he continue to summon up such affection from so many Canadians?

The first fact of Diefenbaker's greatness was that he reached that part of our population which feels excluded from politics. There are about 25 per cent of our population who think of politics as something carried on by "them" for "their" benefit. (Perhaps in a technological

era this percentage will grow, particularly among the dispossessed young.)

In some mysterious fashion Diefenbaker reached those excluded and inarticulate people and persuaded them that he was on their side. What was surprising to political analysts was that he did this as leader of the Conservatives when socialists were not able to achieve that identification. He did this despite the formality of his dress and manners in public. He still wore Homburg hats and elegantly formal suits. I suppose he did it finally because he really did care for all kinds of people in their authentic individuality. The excluded and the inarticulate recognized this, and responded. He was indeed an honest politician; he was a democrat not only in theory but in his soul.

Diefenbaker's principles were grounded in primary loyalties, and loyalty is the great virtue for political leaders. That it is a virtue is often denied in modern political thinking. Intellectuals are apt to believe that leaders should have well thought out "philosophies," which have arisen by putting all primary loyalties in question. But this is nonsense for the following reason.

The virtues necessary for the political life are not altogether the same as those necessary for the contemplative life. The latter requires that one be open to everything, and this includes putting everything in question.

In the practical life one is continually faced with making moral decisions, and in doing so one must not put one's fundamental principles in question, because that only leads to callous opportunism. Diefenbaker's strength was that his fundamental principles were loyalties which he did not put in question. He did not debate his beliefs in freedom within the law, patriotism, social egalitarianism. He just lived them out as best he could. People therefore knew where they stood with him and loved him for it.

In the fast changing world of calculation "loyalty" is often considered outdated and useless for administration. It is therefore becoming a rare virtue in our society. But people were wise to recognize it in Diefenbaker and knew they could rely on him.

Diefenbaker's loyalties came straight out of our particular Canadian tradition. Take his populism as an example. It has been said that Diefenbaker was simply a Canadian William Jennings Bryan, with his appeal to "the people" against the big interests in the east. But that misses the distinctly Canadian flavour of Dief's populism. It misses the fact that he combined his populism with the British tradition of the primacy and nobility of law.

In the opening of the West, individuals went first in the United States and made their own law, in Canada the federal Government went before the immigrants, and the immigrants inherited a tradition of law. Diefenbaker was part of our tradition. He advocated populism, he believed in the rights of individuals, but always within the primacy of law. This was why he gave such strong loyalty to the crown and to Parliament. Like Macdonald he did not see our democracy as a pale imitator of the American, but as something richer, because it understood better the dependence of freedom upon law.

Diefenbaker's nationalism was not ideological; he just took it for granted. It was something given — just as parents are given, both for good and for ill. Because it was not something he constructed as he went along, it had real bite. After all, the nuclear arms crisis of 1963 was the first time since 1935 that a Canadian government really offended the Government of the United States, so that it directly entered Canadian politics. (The next time could be if a Canadian government were to find itself forced over energy.)

But Diefenbaker was speaking honestly when he said: "I am pro-Canadian, not anti-American." He was much too aware of what a dangerous and complex world it is to be ideologically anti-American. He was much too rooted in every day life, in Prince Albert and Ottawa, not to belong to the continent we share with the Americans. He just assumed that Canada is our own, and that the United States is not. He assumed that if we have any pride in our own we must be in some sense sovereign.

When John F. Kennedy told Diefenbaker in Ottawa that Canada could not sell wheat to China — and he meant "could not" quite literally — Diefenbaker replied: "You aren't in Massachusetts now Mr. President." He was expressing that Canadians must take for granted their sovereignty or else have no pride. This was of course a much less worldly-wise assumption than Pearson's recognition that we are finally part of the American empire. Nevertheless it is a necessary basis if we mean anything more than rhetoric about Canada being our country.

Because Diefenbaker's nationalism was a given loyalty, it often showed inadequacies when he tried to express it in office. He was not able to formulate feasible policies necessary to that nationalism in a technological era. But to be fair to him: who since his day has been able to formulate such feasible policies? Even the wisest patriot of this era, de Gaulle, was not able to prevent France being integrated into the homogenized modern culture.

The great criticism of Diefenbaker was always that he was "out of date." In his last years when he had become a respected elder statesman, no longer to be feared, this criticism became a kind of patronizing of him as a fine old dear who was really irrelevant. I always found it unpleasant that Trudeau used to patronize him from this superior standpoint.

But Diefenbaker's loyalties were not defined within such a context of calculation. Indeed it is not surprising that his greatest political humiliation should have been arranged by a public relations executive —

the very type of job which incarnates the absoluteness of calculation.

That is why Diefenbaker was so loved by many of my generation — particularly by those of us less clever and less successful. Despite all his bombast, all his egocentricity, all the wild failures of his judgment, one sensed in him a hold on certain principles which cannot be "out of date" because their truth does not depend upon dates. Despite his almost juvenile engrossment in the day to day excitement of the political scene, one sensed some deep hold on certain good things that do not change. About such good things there has to be calculation, but their essence is beyond all bargaining. It is to be hoped that the political scene will continue to allow such men to be produced.

The cadence of Milton's poetry is not the greatest in the English language, but it is very great. It can catch the rhetoric, the tensions and the nobilities of the battling Baptist lawyer from the prairies.

*Among innumerable false, unmoved Unshaken, unseduced, unterrified.*

Not everybody is false in the modern world, but there are great pressures on all of us in that direction. At the political level Diefenbaker was always a lesson. Whatever else he may have been, he was not false.

— George Grant
Thursday, August 23, 1979
(George Grant is the author
of *Lament for a Nation* and
*Technology and Empire.*)

"**Canada has lost** a man of great stature. As a statesman, politician and public servant, he never wavered. He was unfailing in his loyalty to his country and to the Crown."

> — *Queen Elizabeth II*
> *August 17, 1979*

"**John Diefenbaker did** not tiptoe through the public life of Canada, he strode through, and as he offered passion to his fellow Canadians, he drew passion in return."

> — *Joe Clark*
> *Eulogy at Diefenbaker's burial*
> *Saskatoon, Sask.*
> *August 22, 1979*

"**A lot of** history goes with John Diefenbaker."

> — *Pierre Elliott Trudeau*
> *(on learning of Diefenbaker's death)*
> *August 16, 1979*

"**The Leader of** the Opposition (Mr. Trudeau) suggested his spirit will stay within this room. That, I am sure, is true. But I would like to lay aside, once and for all, a rumour which was quite widely circulated in the west. The rumour that something would happen at the tomb on the third day is completely false. I can vouch for that because I actually live only about 250 yards from the tomb of Mr. Diefenbaker. I am watching it carefully."

> — *Bob Ogle*
> *member for Saskatoon East*
> *House of Commons*
> *October 15, 1979*

*McNALLY*
*MONTREAL STAR, SEPTEMBER, 1967*

# BIBLIOGRAPHY

Where no printed source is cited for a particular quote, the quote has come from the scrapbooks and speeches of John Diefenbaker held in The Right Honourable John G. Diefenbaker Centre.

Bond, Anthony and Shaw, Brian, eds. *Quotations from Chairman Diefenbaker*. Winnipeg: Greywood Publishing, 1968.

Bothwell, Robert; Drummond, Ian; and English, John. *Canada Since 1945: Power, Politics and Provincialism*. Toronto: University of Toronto Press, 1981.

Bothwell, Robert and Kilbourn, William. *C.D. Howe: A Biography*. Toronto: McClelland and Stewart, 1979.

Columbo, John Robert. *Columbo's Canadian Quotations*. Edmonton: Hurtig Publishers, 1974.

Creighton, Donald. *The Forked Road: Canada 1939–1957*. Toronto: McClelland and Stewart, 1976.

Creighton, Donald. *Towards the Discovery of Canada: Selected Essays*. Toronto: Macmillan of Canada, 1972.

Desbarats, Peter and Mosher, Terry. *The Hecklers: A History of Canadian Political Cartooning*. Toronto: McClelland and Stewart, 1979.

Diefenbaker, John G. *One Canada: The Crusading Years 1895–1956*. Toronto: Macmillan of Canada, 1975.

—— *One Canada: The Years of Achievement 1956–1962*. Toronto: Macmillan of Canada, 1976.

—— *One Canada: The Tumultuous Years 1962–1967*. Toronto: Macmillan of Canada, 1977.

Gwyn, Richard. *The Shape of Scandal: A Study of Government in Crisis*. Toronto: Clarke, Irwin and Company, 1965.

Johnston, James. *The Party's Over*. Don Mills: Longman Canada, 1971.

Kendle, John. *John Bracken: A Political Biography*. Toronto: University of Toronto Press, 1979.

Lewis, David. *The Good Fight: Political Memoirs 1909–1958*. Toronto: Macmillan of Canada, 1981.

Macmillan, Harold. *Pointing the Way, 1959–1961*. London: Macmillan, 1972.

Macquarrie, Heath. *The Conservative Party*. Toronto: McClelland and Stewart, 1965.

McKenna, Brian and Purcell, Susan. *Drapeau*. Toronto: Clarke, Irwin and Company, 1980.

Martin, Paul. *Far From Home*. Ottawa: Deneau Publishers, 1983.

Meisel, John. *The Canadian General Election of 1957*. Toronto: University of Toronto Press, 1962.

Morton, Desmond. *A Short History of Canada*. Edmonton: Hurtig Publishers, 1982.

Munro, John, ed. *Wit and Wisdom of John Diefenbaker*. Edmonton: Hurtig Publishers, 1982.

Newman, Peter C. *Distemper of Our Times*. Toronto: McClelland and Stewart, 1968.

Newman, Peter C. *Renegade in Power: The Diefenbaker Years*. Toronto: McClelland and Stewart, 1973.

Nicholson, Patrick. *Vision and Indecision*. Don Mills: Longman Canada, 1968.

Pearson, Lester B. (John Munro and Alex Inglis, eds.) *Mike*: Vol. 3, *1957–1968*. Toronto: University of Toronto Press, 1975.

Pickersgill, J.W. and Forster, D.F. *The Mackenzie King Record*: Vol. 4, *1947–48*. Toronto: University of Toronto Press, 1970.

Roberts, Leslie. *C.D.: The Life and Times of Clarence Decatur Howe*. Toronto: Clarke, Irwin and Company, 1957.

Ross, J. Allan. *Grassroots Prime Minister*. Self-published, no date.

Sevigny, Pierre. *This Game of Politics*. Toronto: McClelland and Stewart, 1965.

Smallwood, Joey. *I Chose Canada: The Memoirs of the Honourable Joseph R. Smallwood*. Toronto: Macmillan of Canada, 1973.

Sorensen, Theodore C. *Kennedy*. New York: Harper and Row, 1965.

Stevens, Geoffrey. *Stanfield*. Toronto: McClelland and Stewart, 1973.

Stursberg, Peter. *Diefenbaker: Leadership Gained 1956–62*. Toronto: University of Toronto, 1975.

—— *Diefenbaker: Leadership Lost 1962–67*. Toronto: University of Toronto, 1976.

Stursberg, Peter. *Lester Pearson and the Dream of Unity*. Toronto: Doubleday Canada Limited, 1978.

Van Dusen, Thomas. *The Chief*. Toronto: McGraw Hill Company of Canada, 1968.

Weir, Carolyn. *Diefenbaker: A Pictorial Tribute*. Toronto: Macmillan of Canada, 1980.

Wente, Margaret, ed. *I Never Say Anything Provocative*. Toronto: Peter Martin Associates, 1975.

Woodcock, George. *Canada and the Canadians*. Toronto: Macmillan of Canada, 1970.

# INDEX OF CARTOONISTS

## "SO LONG, OLD FRIEND"